The GIRLS of GLAMOUR

A GUIDE TO BEING A GODDESS

WRITTEN BY SALLY JEFFRIE
ILLUSTRATED BY NELLIE RYAN
EDITED BY LIZ SCOGGINS
DESIGNED BY ZOE QUAYLE

The GIRLS' BOOK of GLAMOUR

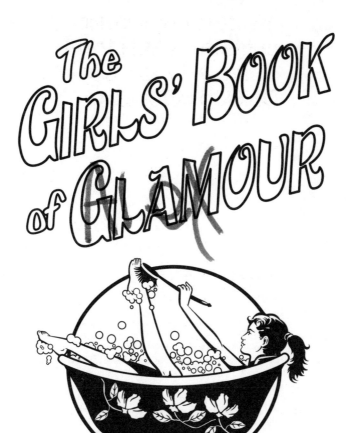

A GUIDE TO BEING A GODDESS

BUSTER BOOKS

For the lovely Kate Jeffrie

First published in Great Britain in 2008 by Buster Books,
an imprint of Michael O'Mara Books Limited,
9 Lion Yard, Tremadoc Road, London SW4 7NQ

www.mombooks.com/busterbooks

Text and illustrations copyright © Buster Books 2008
Cover design by Angie Allison (from an original design by www.blacksheep-uk.com)
Cover illustration: Paul Moran

A CIP catalogue record for this book is available from
the British Library.

ISBN: 978-1-906082-28-4

2 4 6 8 10 9 7 5 3

Printed and bound in England by Clays Ltd, St Ives plc

Papers used by Michael O'Mara Books are natural, recyclable products
made from wood grown in sustainable forests. The manufacturing processes
conform to the environmental regulations of the country of origin.

CONTENTS

NOTE TO READERS

HOW TO MAKE A GOOD FIRST IMPRESSION

First impressions usually last so follow these pointers to make everyone's first thoughts of you the best they can be.

- Remember to introduce yourself and ask the other person's name.

- Look them in the eye, smile and remember to speak clearly.

- Pay attention to what the other person is saying.

- Ask questions about their interests and hobbies.

- Just be yourself.

HOW TO TAKE A COMPLIMENT

There's nothing like receiving dozens of compliments to build up your confidence, even if you flush with embarrassment at first. It's a good idea to use these top tips for the next time a friend says something lovely about you.

- DO smile and say 'thank you'.

- DO be modest.

- DO compliment them in return.

- DON'T frown, mumble or look at the floor.

- DON'T just say 'I know'.

- DON'T disagree.

HOW TO DESCEND A STAIRCASE

A vital part of glamour is impressing people and there's no better way than with a grand entrance. Whether you're arriving at a ball or just trying to wow your friends at school, descending a staircase with style and grace can make a great impression. Here are some pointers for making the best entrance ever – and avoiding any embarrassing slips, trips or falls.

• Pause at the top of the stairs and gaze confidently around the room for a few seconds until everyone turns to look at you. This way you are sure to make maximum impact.

• Discreetly check the staircase ahead for any obvious hazards or obstacles before you take a step.

• If you are in a long ballgown, make sure you lift up the bottom of your dress so you don't tumble.

• Lift up your chin, smile and then lightly grip the handrail to help you keep your balance.

• Step gracefully out onto the first stair, keep smiling and remember not to look at your feet.

• Walk carefully and steadily down the stairs until you reach the bottom. *Voilà.*

HOW TO FLATTER A FRIEND

An essential part of glamour is making other people feel great about themselves, too. So don't just focus on yourself – add an aura of niceness to your personality. Remember to compliment your friends and classmates on their best qualities and you'll soon see how good it makes them feel about themselves.

THINGS YOU SHOULD SAY

- 'Your hair looks lovely.'
- 'I love your drawings.'
- 'You're really talented.'
- 'That really compliments your eyes.'
- 'You've got really nice handwriting.'
- 'You're so well coordinated.'
- 'You're so good at sport.'

THINGS YOU SHOULDN'T SAY

- 'That's so last season.'
- 'Get with the programme!'
- 'You shouldn't wear that colour again.'
- 'What on Earth are you wearing?'
- 'Hahahahahaha.'

HOW TO CUSTOMISE YOUR SCHOOL UNIFORM WITHOUT YOUR TEACHER NOTICING

It is possible to express your own style even if you have to wear a school uniform. Here's how to do it without risking a detention.

• Find out about your school's uniform policy and check it thoroughly for any loopholes. How much you'll be able to customise your uniform depends on how strict your school is. Don't go too far and risk detention!

• Most schools don't insist you wear a particular size or length – within reason. For instance, if you like loose clothes then opt for a blazer in a slightly larger size so it hangs in a baggy style.

• If you have to wear a tie, think about how you'll wear it – perhaps you'd like it very short with a fat knot, or maybe you'd prefer it long with a thin knot. Experiment.

• Check out sales of second-hand school uniforms – most schools have them yearly. Designs of school uniforms subtly change over the years and you might prefer the vintage style of a second-hand item to the new ones currently in the shops.

• Investigate which items you're allowed to choose for yourself and then really express your taste with them. For instance, backpacks can be transformed with a clutch of decorative key rings, shoes can be updated by adding coloured laces and a new hairstyle can be created with different clips and grips.

• If your school only insists that you wear certain colours rather than specific items of clothing, you're really in luck. You'll be

able to experiment with a wide variety of great styles
while sticking to the colour rule.

• Get to know when your teachers are most likely to enforce
uniform rules. For instance, it may be fine to look a bit more
casual at break time so long as you smarten up for assembly.

• Remember – it's definitely your personality, not what
you wear, that really matters.

HOW TO EAT YOUR WAY TO BEAUTIFUL SKIN

Lotions and potions are great and smell lovely, but the very best way to get beautiful skin is from the inside out, which means eating a skin-friendly, healthy diet.

WATER WORKS

You should drink plenty of water throughout the day to keep your skin clear and bright. Aim for about six glasses a day to keep your levels topped up and avoid any fizzy drinks, which are full of sugar.

FRESH AND FRUITY

You should try to eat at least five portions of fresh fruit and vegetables every day. Skin-friendly superfoods include carrots, broccoli, apricots, strawberries, watercress and oranges. They're great for the rest of your body, too.

GREAT NEWS!

Experts can't find any evidence to link eating chocolate with having problem skin, so you can still indulge in the occasional choc-attack.

PERFECT DAILY MEAL PLAN

It's important not to skip meals – a regular, healthy diet can work wonders on your skin and give you lots of energy.

Breakfast. Start with a glass of fresh juice, wholegrain cereal with chopped banana and milk, followed by toast and honey.

Lunch. Make a cheese or ham sandwich on wholemeal bread with salad followed by yoghurt and fruit.

Dinner. Go for grilled chicken and a baked potato with fresh vegetables, followed by fresh fruit salad with yoghurt and nuts.

Snacks. Don't go hungry between meals. If you feel peckish try a healthy snack to keep you going. Fruit, nuts, vegetable sticks, crackers, yoghurt or a slice of wholemeal toast are far better for you than sweets or crisps.

HOW TO MAKE YOUR OWN LIP GLOSS

To give your lips a delicious glow you need a great lip gloss, but there's no need to spend a fortune – it's easy to make your own.

Gather together the following ingredients:

- 30 ml/2 tablespoons of petroleum jelly
- 5 ml/about 1 teaspoon runny honey
- 2 drops food flavouring – peppermint, strawberry or vanilla are particularly good
- A sprinkle of ultra-fine glitter from an art and craft shop (optional).

Mix all the ingredients together until thoroughly blended. Transfer the mixture to a small, clean pot or jar and apply regularly to your lips for a stunning shine.

HOW TO PUT ON A FASHION SHOW

This is a really glamorous way for you and your friends to fill a rainy afternoon. Get everyone to bring a selection of their favourite clothes, accessories and jewellery. Then take it in turns being the stylist, model and photographer at your own catwalk show.

You'll need:

• A camera.

• A great soundtrack you can strut your stuff to.

• Some adults to watch the final show (optional).

THE STYLIST'S JOB

• Select a stunning outfit for your model to wear.

• Chew gum and talk loudly on your mobile phone.

• Wear enormous sunglasses while you dress your model.

THE MODEL'S JOB

- Chew gum, talk on your mobile and demand things.

- Look bored while reading an important work of literature.

- Perfect your 'model walk' – head high, shoulders back, placing one foot directly in front of the other as though you're walking a tightrope.

- Most importantly, never smile.

THE PHOTOGRAPHER'S JOB

- Talk to the model as you take her photograph saying things like 'Love the camera, darling', 'That outfit looks divine' and 'Look this way, this way – wonderful!'

THE FINAL SHOW

Set up a 'catwalk' in the living room with chairs or cushions either side for your audience. Allow the audience in, get the music playing and send your model up the catwalk while the photographer takes shots of her and the audience applauds wildly.

HOW TO GET THE SHINIEST HAIR EVER

If your hair's looking dull and dirty, it's time to take some action. A few extra treats will soon have it back to its shiny, healthy best.

- **Be A Water Baby.** Just as drinking lots of water can help brighten your skin, a good dose of H_2O can keep your hair shiny, too.

- **Little And Often.** If your hair is looking less than glamorous lather up regularly with a mild shampoo to keep the dirt at bay.

- **Shampoo Dry Hair.** If your hair is ultra-dirty try applying the shampoo straight onto dry hair – leave for a couple of minutes before you get to work with water.

- **Get Conditioning.** Condition your hair regularly to guarantee silky, shiny tresses. This easy recipe works really well and saves you valuable cash.

You'll need:

- 5 ml/1 teaspoon of runny honey
- A dash of vinegar
- 50 ml/3 tablespoons evaporated milk.

Mix the ingredients together in a bowl and cover your hair from root to tip. Wind a warm towel around your head and wait for 20 minutes before rinsing thoroughly. The milk will cleanse your hair, while the honey nourishes and the vinegar adds a gloss. Yummy.

- **Rinse, Rinse, Rinse.** Rinse your hair under the shower until the water runs completely clear to be sure no shampoo or conditioner is left behind – it will just make your hair look dull and drab again.

- **Get Brushing.** Groom your hair once or twice a day to remove built-up dirt and dead skin cells. Always brush thoroughly before you wash your hair to allow the shampoo to move easily through it.

Top tip. There's no point brushing your shiny hair with a dirty brush. Wash your brushes and combs regularly in a bowl of warm water with a dollop of shampoo and leave them to dry on a towel.

HOW TO AIR KISS

Make sure you make a cool impression when you bump into friends. It's time to perfect the celebrity-style 'air kiss'.

Start by making sure that you look delighted to see your friend. Smile and widen your eyes and exclaim at how lovely she looks saying 'Darling', 'Honey' and 'Sweetheart' at the same time. Finally swoop towards her and almost touch her left cheek with yours and then her right cheek while saying 'Mwah' loudly each time.

HOW TO MAKE YOUR OWN BUBBLE BATH

Bubbles make a bath a special treat and you can save money by making your own.

Mix together 120 ml/½ cup of baby shampoo, 180 ml/¾ cup of water and a few pinches of salt. Finally, stir in a few drops of essential oil (lavender, lemon or peppermint are especially nice).

Pour the mixture into a pretty bottle. Try to find a plastic one, which won't break if you drop it. Decorate the bottle with stickers and a pretty ribbon and enjoy your bath!

HOW TO TURN BATHTIME INTO A RELAXING TREAT

This bubble-icious bath is best taken just before bed. Get all your chores and homework done first so you can R-E-L-A-X.

SET THE SCENE

- Make sure the bathroom is warm with clean towels ready.

- Have a cup of juice or water nearby, ready to sip as you soak.

- Put on some music and light a scented candle – a lavender one smells especially delicious and is very relaxing.

• Add a little scented bubble bath or oil to the running water – but take care not to leave the bath slippery for the next person.

Top tip. The heads of flowers floating on the surface of the water add a serious touch of glamour.

R-E-L-A-X

Sink into the water and lie there for 20 minutes. Rest your head on a bath cushion or a rolled-up towel and breathe slowly and deeply. Lie there and imagine all the worries of your day dissolving into the water.

AFTERWARDS

Pat your skin dry with a warm, soft towel. Smooth your skin with a little scented body lotion, taking special care of really dry areas like knees and elbows. Pull on your PJs and head straight for bed. Sprinkle a couple of drops of lavender oil on to your pillow to help you drop off.

HOW TO PERSUADE YOUR BEST FRIEND TO LEND YOU HER CLOTHES

A clever way to DOUBLE the size of your wardrobe is to share clothes with a friend. However, if your most stylish friend doesn't seem keen on letting you borrow her clothes, you need to learn how to use the art of persuasion...

- Compliment her on her brilliant taste in clothes and stress how much you'd love to be as well-dressed as her.

- Explain that you'd like to experiment with clothes more but you don't have enough money to buy lots of new things.

- Offer to let her take her pick of your wardrobe if she'll lend you something in return. (If you haven't got many clothes it may be best to wait until your friend has agreed to swap before you let her see the contents of your wardrobe.)

- Promise to wash and iron her clothes before you give them back to her. You will even dry-clean them, if necessary.

- Promise to give her clothes back on an agreed date – and stick to that date to ensure she's happy to swap with you again.

Top tip. Be very careful with your friend's clothes – if you ruin them she'll never let you borrow anything again.

HOW TO QUICKLY SMOOTH AWAY DRY HANDS

Keep a tube of hand lotion by your bedside at all times and remember to apply a drop every morning and evening to keep your skin soft and smooth. But, if your skin is still very dry, try this mini treat:

1. Run yourself a warm bath.

2. Cover your hands in oil – olive oil from the kitchen is fine, although manicurists prefer almond oil. Take the time to rub the oil into your nails, too, as it will help them to grow stronger.

3. Smooth on lots of rich hand lotion – it'll create a barrier around the oil and encourage it to sink into your skin.

4. Now soak in the bath for 10 minutes, allowing your hands to rest in the water.

5. When you get out of the bath, gently rub your hands dry, then apply a few more drops of hand lotion.

You'll be amazed at the results!

HOW TO APPLY EYE-SHADOW

When you're ready to start experimenting with make-up it's a good idea to practise your technique at home before you unleash your new look on the world. Look for flattering, natural shades in a powder finish to highlight the colour of your eyes:

Blue eyes... pastel pinks or peach shades

Brown eyes... olive green or golden brown

Green eyes... lilac or gold

Hazel eyes... greys and mauve.

Make sure your parents are happy for you to try make-up and then start saving your pocket money for your favourite colours. Most make-up ranges offer eyeshadows in sets of three shades, which makes it even easier to find great colours to suit you.

Start with a little of the palest shade to highlight your brow line. Next brush the medium shade across your eyelid, avoiding the inner corner. Then use the darkest colour around the crease of your eye socket to define the shape of your eye. Blend the colours where they meet. Easy peasy.

Brow line

Corner

Crease

Eyelid

HOW TO DEAL WITH ZITS

Even supermodels sometimes get spots. However, with a little know-how you can help a spot to heal quickly and make it almost invisible to the naked eye. Here's the low-down...

HOW TO CURE A SPOT

Firstly, you should NEVER squeeze a spot – it'll just look even more red and inflamed. What's more, you'll risk pushing the infection deeper into your skin and it may leave a permanent scar.

1. Wash your skin thoroughly and pat dry with a clean towel.

2. Wrap an ice cube in a clean hanky and hold it over the spot for a minute or two – it'll help bring down the swelling.

3. Dip the end of a cotton bud into some diluted tea tree oil (available from your chemist) and dot a tiny amount directly onto the spot.

4. Leave it alone to get better.

Top tip. If you keep getting spots in the same area, check they are not being triggered by contact with a telephone, cycle helmet or sunglasses, which aren't spotlessly clean. Check they are not caused by leaning on your hands.

HOW TO USE CONCEALER

Concealers are a great way to cover spots and blemishes so your skin looks perfect. You can buy them from the make-up counter at most chemists and department stores. Don't choose one that's darker or lighter than your natural skin-tone – you'll draw more attention to the problem.

1. If the spot's dry and crusty, apply a little petroleum jelly first to soften it.

2. Apply the concealer to the spot using a clean cotton bud. (Don't apply concealer on areas around the spot that don't need it or you'll just create a 'halo effect'.)

3. Pat some face powder over the concealer to set it and help it stay put all day long.

Top tip. Don't apply concealer with your fingers or you'll risk spreading infection.

IMPORTANT INFORMATION

If you feel you might be suffering from acne rather than just the occasional spot, make an appointment with your family doctor to ask for advice.

HOW TO MAKE
YOUR OWN BODY GLITTER

This fabulous gel can be smoothed onto your body to make your skin shimmer. You can even smooth it through your hair for a gorgeous night-time glow.

What you'll need:

- 5 ml/1 teaspoon of petroleum jelly.
- 20 ml/4 teaspoons aloe vera gel. Aloe vera gel is used to soothe sunburnt or sore skin – it's easy to find in chemists and healthfood stores.

- Ultra-fine glitter (try art and craft stores).
- A small jar. Baby food jars or spice pots are ideal. Make sure they are thoroughly washed out in soapy water.
- A small bowl.
- A spoon.

How to make it:

1. Spoon the aloe vera gel into the bowl. Add the petroleum jelly to make it a little thicker. Stir well.

2. Sprinkle a few pinches of glitter into your mixture. Stir well.

3. Smooth a little onto the back of your hand to see if you like the effect.

4. If it's too glittery, add a little more aloe vera gel. If it's not glittery enough, add an extra pinch of glitter.

5. Keep going until you like the results.

6. Spoon the mixture into your jar.

7. Smooth on the glitter whenever you like and glow, glow, glow!

HOW TO HAIL A BLACK CAB SUCCESSFULLY

If you and your family have taken a trip to the city you may need to hail a cab to get home. Follow these top tips and impress everyone with your incredible cab-hailing skills.

1. Make sure that someone in the family has plenty of cash to pay for the journey.

2. Stand out. Wearing bright colours will help. Stand confidently near the edge of the pavement in a spot where you and your family are easy to see from the road.

3. Keep an eye on the road ahead for the next available taxi. Usually there will be a light on top of the car showing that the cab is not taken by another passenger.

4. As soon as you spot a cab raise your arm and wave elegantly to catch the driver's attention. Never step into the road as this is dangerous. Wait for the taxi to pull over to you.

5. Get into the cab and tell the driver your destination.

6. Sit back and relax. Perfect – your parents are impressed and you are nearly home.

(Make sure you only take a taxi when you are with your family and friends. It is safer that way and you have a ready-made audience to wow.)

HOW TO MAKE YOUR CLOTHES SMELL NICE

Never, ever mix up clean clothes and dirty ones. Put dirty clothes straight into a laundry bag or basket, ready for washing.

- Air your clothes at the end of each day by putting them on a clothes hanger or the back of a chair near an open window. Pop your shoes on the windowsill at the same time – it will help to prevent any unpleasant smells developing.

- Put scented tumble-dryer sheets into your shoes when you're not wearing them to keep them smelling fresh.

- Unwrap a bar of scented soap and place it in the bottom of your wardrobe as an instant clothes freshener.

- Add a few drops of perfume to the final rinse when washing your favourite woollies. They'll smell gorgeous when you snuggle into them.

HOW TO JAZZ UP A BORING PONYTAIL

A simple ponytail can be morphed into lots of new styles. With a little know-how and some practice you'll soon have the best ponytail around.

WRAP IT

Pull a strand of hair out of the ponytail. Wrap it around the top of your ponytail until the hair elastic is hidden. Secure in place with a hair clip.

KNOT IT

Separate your ponytail into six to eight strands. Twist each strand around and around until it forms a loose knot. Pin each knot randomly onto the back of your head.

CURL IT

Curl the ends of your ponytail with self-sticking rollers. Simply twist the rollers into slightly damp hair and leave them in until it's dry. When you remove the rollers, spritz the curls with hairspray to help them last for ages.

CRIMP IT

Pull a few random strands of hair loose from the ponytail. Crimp them with a heated crimping iron then let the tendrils fall around your face

PLAIT IT

Simply plait a ponytail and secure the end with a hair elastic or pretty hair bobble.

ACCESSORISE IT

Grab some pretty clips, hair snaps or other hair jewels and attach them all around the base of your ponytail. Alternatively, brush your hair into a low-slung ponytail at the nape of your neck. Tuck a few feathers – peacock feathers are fantastic – into the hair elastic.

DIP IT

Grab a sachet of temporary hair dye (the sort that washes out straight away – not permanent or semi-permanent). Follow the instructions on the packet carefully but only apply the dye to the ends of your hair. It should look as though your ponytail has been dipped in colour. Experiment with funky colours – black, red or orange are great with this look.

HOW TO HAVE A GOOD NIGHT'S SLEEP

A good night's sleep helps you feel great and look gorgeous. Most glamorous girls need around ten hours sleep each night. Try this mini bedtime routine to help you float off to the Land of Nod.

HAVE A LIGHT SNACK

Sweet treats, heavy meals and sugary drinks just before bed will keep you awake. If your tummy's rumbling, have some warm milk, a banana or a slice of wholemeal toast an hour before bed. A cup of peppermint or chamomile tea will help you relax, too.

WIND DOWN

Try to relax during the hour before bed by reading a book or listening to some gentle music. Make sure you get your homework done earlier in the evening – doing it just before bed will leave your mind racing and keep you awake.

ENSURE YOUR BEDROOM'S DARK AND QUIET

Make sure the curtains are pulled tight and ban any ticking clocks. If you live in a noisy household, make a 'Do Not Disturb' sign for your bedroom door and use it.

PREPARE FOR BED

Put a glass of water by your bed in case you wake up thirsty. Pull on some comfy PJs, wash your face, clean your teeth and hop between the sheets. Read for a while until you feel nice and sleepy then turn out the light.

GET COMFORTABLE

Make sure your neck is well-supported with one or two soft pillows. Don't wrap yourself up in too many blankets – you don't want to get too hot in the night.

LET YOUR WORRIES FLOAT AWAY

Worrying can keep you awake. If you're anxious about something, try this trick: Imagine you're putting the problem into a box. Then imagine you're putting the box into a cupboard and locking it away till morning. This often helps you relax enough to drop off.

Good night...

HOW TO BATHE LIKE CLEOPATRA

Cleopatra, the queen of Ancient Egypt, was said to bathe in milk. You too can take a milk bath to soothe and soften your skin.

Just add two pints of whole milk to a tub of warm water. Swirl it around thoroughly, so that the water goes white. Hop in and have a good soak for at least 20 minutes. Rinse in clear cool water.

HOW TO DO A PERFECT PIROUETTE

Find a good place to practise your pirouette. Carpets are not good at all so try the tiles in your kitchen or bathroom. Make sure there's enough space that if you fall you won't crash into something and hurt yourself.

Start with your left foot turned out and the heel of your right foot against the toes. This is called 'fifth position'.

Lift your right arm as though you are hugging a beach ball to your chest and hold your left arm out to the side, slightly curved towards your body.

Then the difficult bit. Keep your back straight and in one movement bend your knees outwards in a *'plié'*, push up onto the tiptoes of your left foot and bring your right foot up to your knee with your toes pointed. At the same time use your momentum to spin clockwise.

When you have turned full circle, lower yourself off tiptoes onto your left foot and bring your right leg back into its original 'fifth position'. Always take the weight of your body on your supporting leg when you finish your pirouette.

Top tip. It's a good idea to learn how to 'spot' so that you don't get dizzy spinning around. Practise slowly at first to get the technique just right. Keep your eyes on one 'spot' on the wall. Slowly spin your body round, keeping your head in the same position until you can't turn anymore. Then whip your head around at the last possible second to the same spot again while you continue to turn. Perfect.

HOW TO MAKE
SOAP-ON-A-ROPE

Hanging the soap up in the shower means it's always easy to find – it makes a great gift, too.

You'll need:

- Three bars of white soap
- Cheese grater
- Bowl and jug
- Piece of rope, ribbon or garden twine
- Waxed or greaseproof paper
- Rubber gloves
- Food colouring.

1. Finely grate the soap into a large bowl.

2. Fill the jug with warm water. If you want to make coloured soap, add a few drops of your chosen food colouring to the water – don't over do it though, or you'll find your skin changing colour as you wash!

3. Add drops of the warm water slowly to the soap flakes until it's the consistency of thick porridge.

4. Pull on the rubber gloves and mix well with your hands.

5. Cut the rope, ribbon or twine into your chosen length (30–40 cm is ideal) and lay onto the waxed paper.

6. Pat the soap mixture around one end of the rope in a ball shape, making sure the rope is in the centre of the soap ball.

7. Once you're happy with the shape, leave the soap to dry for around 24 hours.

8. Tie a loop in the other end of the rope so that you can hang it up in the shower.

Top tip. You can add a handful of other ingredients to the soap mixture to ring the changes.

- Dried flowers look and smell very pretty.

- Porridge oats turn a simple soap into an effective body scrub.

- Grated lemon peel makes a refreshing soap that will really wake you up in the morning.

HOW TO GET THE FLUTTERIEST LASHES

A slick of mascara is the best way to create a fluttering fringe to your eyes – especially if you have light-coloured hair and your lashes are harder to notice. Here's what you need to know:

Most mascaras are applied with a spiral brush at the end of a wand as this makes them quick and easy to use. Some contain fibres to add extra thickness and length to your lashes. For a girl on the go, waterproof mascara is the best choice. It will withstand tears, showers and swimming. However, remember you'll need a special make-up remover to take it off as it clings to your lashes more than ordinary mascara.

1. Start by applying mascara to your upper lashes first. Brush them downwards to begin with, then brush the lashes upwards from underneath. Use a tiny zigzag movement from side to side to prevent the mascara turning to lumps on your lashes.

2. With the tip of the mascara wand brush your lower lashes, using a gentle side-to-side technique. You can keep your hand steady by resting your elbow on a firm surface. If you've got a shaky

hand, try holding the edge of a tissue under your eyelashes while applying mascara to prevent it smudging onto your skin.

3. Comb through your lashes with an eyelash comb to remove any small lumps of mascara. This will prevent your lashes from clumping together.

4. Take care not to blink while the mascara is still wet or your lashes will stick together.

5. Repeat the whole process once or twice more to create a really fluttery effect.

HOW TO WORK OUT YOUR FACE SHAPE

Different hairstyles suit different face shapes. The four main face shapes are oval, round, heart-shaped and square.

To work out what shape your face is, pull all your hair back from your face with a hairband. Look in a mirror and trace around the outline of your face with a lipstick (the sharp edge of a bar of soap will work well, too). Move away from the mirror and look carefully at the shape. Decide which shape your face is most similar to, then check out the description and choose from your ideal hairstyles. (Don't forget to clean the mirror afterwards!)

OVAL

Any style suits an oval face so you can try really dramatic looks like ultra-short bobs and 'urchin' crops as well as long, straight hair.

ROUND

HEART-SHAPED

You would suit chin-length bobs,
soft layers or side partings.

SQUARE

Try neat styles with flipped-
up ends. Long wispy fringes,
waves or short and spiky
cuts would also work well
for you.

Go for soft layers, curls,
side-swept partings or hair
swept onto your face.

HOW TO MAKE YOUR EYES LOOK BRIGHTER

If you're feeling tired and you've stared at a computer screen for too long or you're simply fighting off a cold, your eyes might start to look really red. Here's how to make them sparkle again with a simple three-step plan:

1. A lack of water can make your eyes look really tired so drink a litre and a half of water every day to banish redness.

2. Empty an ice cube tray into a sink of cold water and soak a flannel. Wring the cold flannel out, then lie down and place it over your eyes for five minutes. If the flannel gets too warm, soak it in the iced water again and repeat.

3. Apply a dot of pale, pearly eyeshadow on the skin at the inner corner of your eye and just above your pupil. This will make your eyes look wider and brighter even if you're still sleepy.

HOW TO PLAN A THEME PARTY

When it's time to celebrate it can be a great idea for you and your friends to throw a themed party. Get permission from the adults first then plan away.

• Choosing your theme might depend on the season, such as Halloween, Christmas or Summertime fun. Or you can just make one up – good ideas include Think Pink, Superheroes, Hawaiian or Hollywood. You could even base a party theme on your favourite TV show or on a particular era in history – Roman, Egyptian or the 1970s.

• Decide whether it will be a francy dress party or not. Your guests will need time to create their outfits to fit with your theme.

• Send out your invitations in good time and include all the information they need about the theme. Ask people to RSVP (this is French for *'Répondez S'il Vous Plaît'*, which means they need to reply) – this way you'll know how many guests to expect.

• The party decorations should go with your theme – for instance, hollow out pumpkins for Halloween, hang pink balloons and ribbons for a Think Pink party, drape furniture with white sheets and bunches of grapes for a Roman party.

• Keep your guests entertained with plenty of party games and dancing.

• It's a good idea to have music ready to keep the atmosphere lively. If you don't have lots of your own CDs you could ask your guests to bring along their favourites to dance to.

HOW TO MAKE A BAG CHARM

Glam up a plain handbag or a boring old schoolbag with a safety pin bag charm. It couldn't be easier.

What you'll need:

- 30 safety pins, various sizes
- Beads of various sizes
- Piece of thin elastic – about 15 cm

GET BEADING

1. Open up a safety pin. Thread as many beads as you can onto the pin – don't forget to get creative with the pattern.

2. Close the pin carefully.

3. Repeat this process for as many safety pins as you have.

4. Knot a bead on one end of the piece of elastic.

5. Now start threading the beaded safety pins onto the elastic. Thread some through the top end of the pin, some through the bottom end and some through the middle.

6. Finish off with two beads, secured with a knot.

7. Tie the remaining end of the elastic thread around the base of the handle of your bag.

HOW TO GIVE YOURSELF A MINI FACIAL

Every couple of weeks, set aside a bit of time to give yourself a relaxing salon-style facial at home. It'll help keep skin deep-down clean and super soft.

1. Smooth your skin with cleansing cream, gentle soap or facial wash. Leave on for one or two minutes to give it time to dissolve grime and make-up, then smooth away with a clean, damp flannel.

2. Massage a blob of facial scrub or some porridge oats over your skin to whisk away dead surface skin cells and clear blocked pores. Rinse away with warm water.

3. Fill a bowl with a kettleful of freshly boiled water (ask an adult to supervise this part). Then lean over the bowl, capturing the steam by placing a towel over your head. Stay there for five minutes to allow the steam to warm and soften your skin. Sensitive skins should skip this step.

4. Splash your face with warm water and pat dry.

5. Smooth on a home-made fruit face pack.

Oily skins. Crush six strawberries with a fork, smooth onto your face and leave for three minutes.

Normal/dry skins. Crush a peeled banana with a fork, smooth onto your face and leave for five minutes.

6. Remove the mask with a clean tissue then rinse your face with warm water.

7. Finish with a splash of cool water to freshen your skin. Pat dry with a towel.

8. Dot your skin with moisturiser and massage it in to encourage a brighter complexion.

HOW TO TELL A FRIEND SHE'S MADE A FASHION ERROR

Too shy to tell a friend her top is on inside out or her shirt is buttoned up wrongly? Don't be – she'll be less embarrassed if a good friend tells her straight away rather than letting her walk around looking really silly all day long. And you never know when you might need her to do the same favour for you!

Plan ahead. Get together with your friends and make up some subtle hand signals to warn each other – you could tug on your earlobe or sing a snippet from your favourite song. That way you'll know that you have each other's backs just in case the worst happens.

If you haven't prepared in advance for a fatal fashion disaster then the best thing to do is to quickly grab your friend and point out the error in your best quiet voice.

HANDY HINTS

• Compliment your friend on how well she handled the situation.

• Point out how great her taste in clothes is so who cares if anyone laughed?

• Change the subject as soon as you can.

Top tip. Don't actually point. This will only draw attention to the situation and embarrass her more.

THINGS TO AVOID

• Any kind of laughter – this will only draw attention to the problem.

• Telling other people first – this is a quick way to end a friendship.

• Doing an impression of how embarrassed she was.

HOW TO CUSTOMISE A T-SHIRT WITH FABRIC PAINTS

Wear your art on your sleeve as well as on the rest of your T-shirt by getting nifty with some fabric paints. The easiest way to create your own T-shirt design is with fabric pens – they allow you to paint directly onto the fabric without any mixing or mess and you can get them from most art and craft shops.

Here's how:

1. You'll need a plain T-shirt. Choose a plain white or pastel-coloured one so that your design shows up really well.

2. Practise your design on a piece of paper first. You could try graffiti-style, designing your own logo or just drawing a simple, bold image like a face or a sun.

3. Now you're ready to paint your T-shirt. Put a piece of thick paper or card inside the T-shirt so that the ink doesn't leak through from the front to the back.

4. Draw your image straight onto the T-shirt.

5. When you use fabric pens, you need to iron your finished design to help 'set' it. Check with an adult for advice or help before you do this.

Top tip. Once you've invested in a set of fabric pens, you can make use of them on lots of projects. Why not decorate shoe bags or pillowcases?

HOW TO CONVINCE PEOPLE YOU'RE A CELEBRITY

• Wear huge sunglasses that practically cover your whole face even when you're inside the house eating your tea.

• Go to school with a film crew (your kid brother and his friends will do). Explain to your teacher that you're the subject of a brand new reality TV show.

• Carry a huge handbag with a dog the size of a hamster in it.

• Apply fake tan from top to toe until you are bright orange.

• Wear very silly shoes.

• Be unreasonable wherever you go. You could tell the dinner ladies you're on a special diet and can only eat blue food or tell your teacher you didn't finish your homework because you were practising your Oscar acceptance speech.

• Get your parents to tint the windows of the family car.

• Travel with an entourage (a group of friends) at all times to help you with any boring tasks.

HOW TO TURN AN OLD PAIR OF JEANS INTO A FAB SKIRT

Here's the perfect way to recycle an old pair of jeans you don't like anymore into a skirt you'll love.

1. Take the pair of jeans and cut straight across both legs at the length you would like your skirt to be.

2. Cut carefully up the inside seam of each leg and trim off the extra fabric. At the front cut to just below the fly and overlap the curved sections. At the back cut to about 5 cm below the waist band.

3. On a flat surface overlap the curved sections at the front and back and sew into place.

4. From one of the pieces of cast-off legs, cut a triangle large enough to fill the gap between the legs (alternatively, you could use a pretty cotton fabric to contrast with the denim).

5. Either sew the triangles to the insides of the legs by hand or use a sewing machine.

6. Don't bother hemming the bottom of the skirt if you want to wear it straight away – the frayed look is very cool.

Top tip. If you're feeling creative sew a length of ribbon or lace trimming around the hem to add an extra touch of glamour.

HOW TO PERSUADE YOUR PARENTS TO LET YOU HAVE YOUR EARS PIERCED

If you really want to get your ears pierced you need to get permission first. It's worth planning in advance how to get your parents on your side. Whatever you do, don't let a friend pierce your ears for you – it's unhygenic and you'll risk an infection.

- Before you start on your campaign to convince your parents, be sure you really do want your ears pierced – there are some great clip-on earrings available that look just as good.

- Do your research first. The more knowledge you have, the easier it'll be to persuade your parents.

- Offer to pay for it yourself or suggest it would be a great birthday present.

- Visit a couple of ear-piercing shops with your parents first. They will be able to check who would do the procedure and the equipment that's used. Let your parents choose which place they prefer.

- Don't burst into tears or throw a tantrum if they refuse. Leave it for a while and ask again. Perhaps you'll eventually be able to persuade them to set a date when they'll allow you to have your ears pierced.

HOW TO LOOK AFTER NEWLY PIERCED EARS

Pierced ears might look good, but infected ears do not. Here's how to look after your newly pierced lobes properly:

- Make sure your first pair of earrings have gold posts (that's the part of the earring that goes through the hole). Gold posts are less likely to cause infection and swelling.

- When you first get your ears pierced, you should leave the earrings in for six weeks until your ears are completely healed. If you don't, your holes could close up and you'll have to go through everything all over again!

- Don't fiddle with your earrings during this healing process.

- Keep shampoo, soap and hairspray away from your ears.

- Apply antiseptic lotion to your ears morning and night – you should be given some by the person who pierced your ears. Wash your hands first, then apply the lotion to your ears with a clean cotton bud.

- Finally, rotate each earring once every morning and night.

WHAT IF YOUR EARS GET INFECTED?

An infected ear lobe may be swollen, red, warm and painful or oozing fluid. If you think one of your pierced ears may be infected, tell an adult immediately. They'll probably want to check with your family doctor for advice on how to deal with the infection. Follow any advice carefully to ensure your pierced ears become healthy again.

HOW TO SHAMPOO AND CONDITION YOUR HAIR PROPERLY

Scientists have worked out exactly how you should wash and condition your hair. After experimenting on hundreds of people, they came up with the following instructions:

SHAMPOOING

- Dampen your hair with running water warmed to a temperature of precisely 36.7 C°.

- Use exactly the right amount of shampoo – 6 ml of shampoo for short hair, 8 ml for medium length hair and 10 ml for long hair.

- Lather hair for 28 seconds, rubbing it 20 times with your fingertips.

- Rinse your hair for 22 seconds in water that's 36.7 C°.

- Repeat the whole process.

CONDITIONING

- Use 2 ml conditioner for short hair, 4 ml for medium hair and 6 ml for long hair.

- Apply conditioner with a wide-toothed comb.

- Leave the conditioner to sink in for 57 seconds before rinsing with water at 36.7 C°.

- Pat your hair dry with a towel to absorb excess water before leaving it to dry naturally.

You have been told!

HOW TO GET SUPER-SOFT FEET WHILE YOU SLEEP

DID YOU KNOW?

• There are 26 bones in each of your feet.

• Each time your feet hit the floor, double the weight of your body impacts with the floor.

• Over 50% of people don't like their feet, often as a result of foot problems.

• Your feet contain around 250,000 sweat glands and they perspire more than any other part of your body. Each foot produces an egg-cup-full of sweat each day.

• In your lifetime, it's estimated that your feet will carry you 110,000 km or almost three times around the world.

Indulge your feet with the following treat once a week and they'll always be soft and smooth...

1. Rub your feet with a layer of rich foot lotion. If you prefer, you can make your own by mixing 60 ml/¼ cup olive oil, 60 ml/¼ cup single cream and 20 ml/1 tbsp mayonnaise.

2. Pull on a pair of socks and head for bed.

3. Wash off the cream in the morning to reveal beautifully soft tootsies.

4. Don't forget to put the socks in the wash!

HOW TO GROW YOUR NAILS SUCCESSFULLY

If you regularly nibble your nails it's a hard habit to break but well worth trying if you'd like to grow elegantly long and strong nails.

Restrict yourself to biting the nails on just one hand and then on only one nail. You'll soon be inspired to grow out the bitten one.

Regularly apply scented hand lotion or an anti-nail-biting cream. The unpleasant flavour will soon put you off gnawing your nails.

If your parents and school allow it, try using stick-on nails for a few weeks so your nails have a chance to grow underneath.

HEALTHY NAILS

Once you've broken a nail-biting habit follow these pointers to grow the perfect set of pinky tips. The secret to growing your nails is to make sure they are as strong as possible so…

• Eat two portions of protein a day. Meat, fish, dairy, soya and lentils will all help your nails to grow strong and healthy.

• When you wash the dishes make sure you always wear washing-up gloves – soaking your hands in water weakens the nails.

• When your nails begin to grow keep them in shape with a nail file or an emery board to prevent them breaking.

• Make sure your nails are dry, then gently smooth away any rough edges and file them into a nice, even shape.

• Never file down into the sides of your nails – it can lead to infection and seriously weakens your nails.

• Don't use your nails as a tool. Find the right tool for the job rather than risk having to grow your nail from scratch again.

Always file in one direction only, at a 45° angle under the nail.

Never file backwards and forwards – it can cause the nail layers to split

• Once a week, soak your bare nails in a bowl of olive oil for 10 minutes. Then wipe away the excess oil with some cotton wool.

DID YOU KNOW?

• Nails grow about 3 mm a month.

• They grow faster in summer than in winter.

• If you've lost a nail due to an accident, it'll take about six months to grow back.

• Your middle finger grows the quickest while your thumbnail grows the slowest.

• A child's nail grows more quickly than an adult's.

• Toenails grow more slowly than fingernails.

HOW TO CONVINCE PEOPLE YOU'RE A HAND MODEL

Just having beautiful hands isn't enough – you have to act the part properly as well. Following these tips will help convince your friends that your hands are your fortune and provide you with a ready-made excuse for avoiding all sorts of boring tasks.

- Refuse to do anything that might damage your hands. This can include doing the washing-up (dries out the skin), writing essays (you could get ink on your fingers) and taking the dog for a walk (the dog's lead could cause calluses to form on your hands).

- Gather together a handful of props like a lipstick, a cup of coffee and a box of washing powder. Get your best friend to take close-up pictures of your hands holding the props – just like in the adverts. Mount the results in a photograph album and, *voilà*: your very own portfolio to show people.

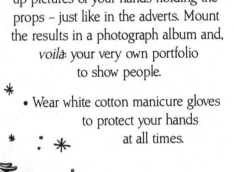

- Wear white cotton manicure gloves to protect your hands at all times.

• Practise hand-modelling poses whenever anyone's around. Don't just pass your mum a magazine she wants to read – strike a 'hand pose' as you do it.

• Take up music lessons. Playing a musical instrument helps to encourage steady hands – vital for photographic shoots, which can go on for hours.

• Insist that you have jelly for pudding after every meal. Hand models say the gelatine in it is good for strengthening nails.

• Change the colour of your nail polish each night – after all, you need a new look for every single photo shoot.

• Get your parents to insure your hands for a million pounds.

HOW TO SHAPE YOUR NAILS TO SUIT YOUR HANDS

When you're filing your nails, make sure you bear in mind your overall hand-shape and pick a file-style that might suit you best.

• If you have small hands – go for almond-shaped nails.

• If you have quite short, wide fingers – aim for 'squoval'-shaped nails (which is just an oval with a squared-off tip).

• If you have large hands or wide nails try squared-off ends.

HOW TO BE THE BEST BRIDESMAID

It's a real honour to be asked to be someone's bridesmaid or flower girl. Here's how to impress the bride on her Big Day.

Smile sweetly when you see your dress for the first time. It doesn't matter if you hate lime-green satin – it's the bride's choice. Just comment on how clever of her it was to match your dress to her bouquet.

Have something to eat and drink before you put on your outfit. That way you won't spoil it with crumbs and you'll have energy to get through the day. It might be a long time before you get a chance to eat again.

Offer to look after younger bridesmaids or flower girls if there are any. Very young children have a habit of playing hide and seek under the bride's dress and bursting into tears during the ceremony.

If the bride has a long skirt and veil, make sure it's all straight before she enters the church or registry office. If you're the oldest bridesmaid, you'll need to take the bride's bouquet during the marriage service, then hand it back to her afterwards.

Offer to help out with small chores during the day such as getting the bride a drink of water while she's getting ready or handing out wedding cake to guests later on.

Most of all, smile and enjoy yourself.

HOW TO WALK WITH CONFIDENCE

The best way to make people think you're brimming with self-assurance and poise is to strut like a star. Follow these steps to get the best out of your stride.

1. Imagine that someone is pulling your head up with a long piece of string, push your shoulders back and smile.

2. Think of a fast-paced, lively song that you love and sing the tune in your head, or out loud if you prefer.

3. Gently start swinging your arms and walk along to the rhythm of your song, bouncing a little at the knees.

4. Heads will turn – just remember to smile and wave.

HOW TO CRY AT A WEDDING

There's nothing like a happy occasion to bring out smiles and tears. Here's how to get your fill of crying without upstaging the bride.

- Take a pretty cotton hanky with you rather than an old tissue – use it to dab gently at your eyes if you start to well up.

- Remember to smile and breathe while you are crying, you don't want to pull scary faces at a wedding.

- It's important not to sob too loudly or blow your nose noisily. This may prevent everyone else from enjoying the ceremony.

- Don't cry for too long or people will start to worry about you rather than thinking how beautiful the bride is.

HOW TO GET RID OF PUFFY EYES

If you've got a cold, hay fever or you're just really tired, try this de-puffing trick.

Stand a clean teaspoon in a glass of iced water. After a few minutes, remove it and hold the spoon against your closed eyes until they feel cooler and brighter.

HOW TO PRETEND YOU'VE GOT FRECKLES

If you have freckles, never try to hide them – they make you look naturally pretty and sun-kissed. If you're not lucky enough to have freckles, there's an easy way to fake them.

1. Start by making sure that your skin is really clean.

2. Choose a light brown eyebrow pencil if you have pale skin and a deeper shade if you have darker skin.

3. Sharpen the eyebrow pencil and dot a few freckles onto your face, concentrating them around your nose and cheeks.

4. To make your fake freckles look more realistic, apply different sized dots and soften the edges with a clean cotton bud.

5. Dust your skin with a little face powder to set them in place.

Top tip. For a speedy way to create an impression just draw on a 'beauty spot'. Take a black eyebrow pencil, and apply a firm dot to your skin about 2 cm from your top lip, then set it with a little face powder.

HOW TO EXIT A LIMO GRACEFULLY

Once you're a celebrity you'll be invited everywhere – and a stretch limousine is definitely the best way to arrive. But when all your fans and photographers are waiting to see you it's important to learn how to get out of the car without falling over yourself.

1. Open the door on the pavement side and check there's room for you to get out easily. Don't let camera flashes distract you.

2. While staying seated swing both feet out onto the pavement. Use the door handle and the frame of the car to gently push yourself up in one smooth movement. Do not rush this stage.

3. Remember to tilt your head forward a little to avoid banging it on the door frame as you stand up straight.

4. Shake out your dress to make sure you haven't wrinkled it then turn towards your waiting fans to smile, wave and head for the red carpet zone.

5. Pause for a moment or two for the waiting photographers and film crews. Don't forget to strike a pose (see page 118).

6. Remember to stop and give a few quick autographs to some of your fans before heading in to your glamorous event.

HOW TO MAKE A RIBBON BELT

Jazz up your tired old jeans with a pretty plaited belt made from lengths of colourful ribbon. Here's how to do it:

1. Look for ribbon that's about 2–3 cm wide.

2. Choose three different colours that all look good together.

3. Measure around your waist. Multiply this measurement by three – that's the length you should cut your ribbons to.

4. Take a strand of each colour. Tie them together in a knot at one end. Lay them on a table and start plaiting. You can plait it loosely or tightly – it's up to you!

5. Tie a knot at the end of the plait.

6. Form two more plaits from the remaining ribbons.

7. Now plait the three plaits together to make a fat ribbon belt. Secure each end with a knot.

8. Simply thread the belt through the loops of your jeans and show off your new style. Tie the two ends together to secure.

Top tip. To create a more glamorous effect just cut the ribbon strands a little longer and leave the ends loose to flutter around. You could even add a selection of pretty, glittery beads for some extra sparkle.

HOW TO CLEAN YOUR MAKE-UP BRUSHES

Make-up brushes are the best way to apply make-up but they can get dirty. Wash them every week or two to keep your brushes clean and your face healthy.

1. Squirt a little shampoo into a cup and top up with warm water.

2. Swish the brushes in the water to dissolve dirt and grime.

3. Rinse the hairs under a running tap until the water runs clear.

4. Gently squeeze the brushes with your fingers to remove excess moisture.

5. Place a clean towel on a flat surface and lay the brushes on top.

6. Leave them to air-dry.

HOW TO MAKE YOUR BEDROOM SKIN-FRIENDLY

Central heating can draw the moisture out of your skin, leaving it dry and dull, but there's a simple way to prevent this happening.

Keep the air moist in your bedroom simply by placing a well-watered houseplant on your windowsill or by keeping a bowl of water near a radiator. This way the water will gradually evaporate and humidify the air, keeping your skin moist.

HOW TO GET THE HAIR YOU REALLY WANT

If you're growing out your hair it can be difficult to avoid a few bad-hair days until you get the style you want. Have a regular trim to snip away split ends and keep your hair looking healthy. Tell your hairdresser what style you're aiming for – they will be able to trim your hair to help you reach your goal as quickly as possible.

It's easy to end up with a haircut you don't like unless you tell your stylist exactly what you want – follow these tips to avoid a really terrible hair day.

• Don't be shy about showing the hairdresser a photograph of the hairstyle you'd like. Be prepared for them to explain that the style might not suit your hair type or face shape – try to find a good compromise.

• Always use your fingers to show the stylist how long you want your hair, how much you want cut off and the shape you're after.

- Don't bury your nose in a magazine while your hair is being cut. Watch what the stylist is doing and politely but firmly stop them if they're about to make a mistake.

- Take a good look in the mirror when they have finished. It's your last chance to point out any problems and give your stylist the opportunity to put things right.

Remember – a good diet, regular exercise and plenty of sleep will encourage your hair to grow more quickly. Experiment with different looks as your hair goes through different lengths and invest in hair clips and hair elastics to add extra style as it grows.

HOW TO GROW OUT YOUR FRINGE

- Start wearing your fringe away from your face straightaway – use clips or a hairband to keep loose tendrils out of your eyes.

- Switch to a side parting so that your fringe still looks stylish as it grows out.

- Consider having some face-framing layers cut into the rest of your hair to help balance out your fringe as it's growing.

HOW TO CREATE YOUR PERSONAL STYLE

Following fashion slavishly can cost a small fortune. Be creative and thrifty and come up with a brilliant style of your very own.

- Look for inspiration in magazines and on TV, then select the things you like most.

- Pick and choose the things you like and imagine how you could combine them into a style of your own.

- Lay all your clothes out in your room and sort them into piles of things that suit you and things you'd like to adapt.

- Try changing the length or adding extra trimming to items that are old and dull.

- Experiment with unusual combinations and try layering or adding accessories.

- Scour second-hand shops for fabulous bargains that suit your style and pick them up cheaply. It's the greenest way to shop because you'll be recycling clothes.

HOW TO ACCESSORISE BRILLIANTLY

You'll be surprised how many accessories you already have lying around at home. Anything from scarves and belts to brooches and bracelets can be used to add instant pizzazz to your wardrobe. Most of these ideas can be achieved with items you already own so you needn't spend any extra money.

• Tie the ends of a long scarf together and hook your left arm into the loop, then bring the scarf across your back and hook your right arm into the other end to make an instant shrug.

• If last year's coat is looking a bit bedraggled jazz it up with a pretty brooch or a fabric flower. Pin it on to a lapel or somewhere just below your collar bone.

• If your hair is misbehaving why not just cover it up? Take a scarf or a pretty top and wrap it around your head like a turban or a bandana. For extra sparkle pin on a glamorous brooch just above your forehead.

• When a cold winter breeze is getting to you simply fold your scarf in half, loop it around your neck and slip the ends through the loop. This will cut out all the draughts and look super-stylish.

• Gather together all of the bangles and bracelets you own and put them all on at once – they'll be very eye-catching and make a great noise at the same time.

• A pretty silk or chiffon scarf can be used for lots of different things – knot it at the neck, tie it at the waist or loop it around your wrist and tie it in a stylish bow.

HOW TO STOP CHLORINE IN SWIMMING POOLS DAMAGING YOUR HAIR

Swimming is a fantastic way to get fit, but it can wreak havoc with your poor hair. That's because the water in most swimming pools contains a chemical called chlorine which kills germs in the water and makes it safe to swim in. The trouble with chlorine, though, is that it can make your hair dull, dry and unmanageable.

• Coat your hair with some conditioner, then pull on a swimming cap to protect it against the chlorine in the pool.

• If you're too vain to wear a swimming cap, make sure you wet your hair under the shower before you get into the water. That way your hair will already be soaked and as a result will absorb much less of the chlorinated water.

• Shampoo your hair as soon as you get out of the pool using a special swimmer's shampoo – this contains ingredients to remove the chlorine from your hair.

• Use loads of conditioner after swimming to guard against the drying effects of chlorine on your hair.

Top tip. Chlorine can actually make blonde hair look a little green. If you have blonde hair and find this happens to you ask an adult to dissolve four soluble aspirin for you in a jug of water. Pour it over your hair and leave for five minutes, before rinsing. The juice of a lemon or a little vinegar in 500 ml/2 cups of water works pretty well, too.

HOW TO HAVE THE PRETTIEST SUMMER FEET

- Get three pretty shades of polish that go well together (pastels work best).

- Apply one coat of the first polish all over your toenails. Allow it to dry.

- Grab the second shade and paint a dot of colour in the centre of each nail.

- Take the last colour and place several dots around the centre, like the petals of a flower.

- Allow the polish to dry.

- Show off your new look by slipping on a pair of pretty flip-flops.

HOW TO HOST A SPA-STYLE PARTY

Impress and pamper your friends by inviting them round for a relaxing and luxurious beauty evening at your place. Ask everyone to bring a dressing gown, flip-flops, hairbands, a mirror and a face cloth.

Get the mood right by covering seats and tables with white sheets. Use lamps or, better still, fairy lights to create a relaxing atmosphere and switch on some calming music. Check out your local library for special CDs that are designed for relaxation (forest or ocean sounds are particularly mellow) for when you're having a foot massage – there are lots around.

Prepare some healthy spa-style snacks and drinks. Sparkling water or fruit juices look good in pretty glasses with colourful straws. Make special ice cubes to add to the drinks the day before. Pop slices of strawberry, lemon or lime into each section of an ice cube tray, then add water and freeze. A selection of fruit, popcorn and little sandwiches are good choices for mini-bites.

Top tip. Snacks on cocktail sticks are a great idea – your guests will find them easier to pick up if they have wet nail polish.

SPA TREATMENTS

Gather together a group of parents or friends to act as spa staff. Get them to set up separate 'beauty stations' offering different treatments. Create a poster board to outline which treatments are available, and let your guests pick the three they would like.

Nifty Nails. File away rough edges from nails with an emery board. Slick on clear nail polish, then sprinkle over some glitter while the polish is still wet. Seal in with a second coat of polish.

Sensational Stripes. Get a tube of 'hair mascara' or some brightly coloured eyelash mascara. Comb it through dry hair for instant, washable highlights. This looks great if you concentrate the colour in the front sections of your guest's hair.

Magical Masks. For each mask, mix together a teaspoon of runny honey, three tablespoons of natural yoghurt and a few drops of lemon juice. Apply to clean skin and pop cucumber slices over the eyes. Relax for five minutes and rinse.

Fruity Feet. Add a few drops of fruit-scented bubble bath to a large bowl of warm water. Get your guest to soak their feet for five minutes. Pat their feet dry then give them a foot massage using a few drops of olive oil or body lotion.

Glamorous Lashes. Start by curling your friend's eyelashes with a metal eyelash curler. Gently does it – take care not to pinch her skin or pull on the lashes. Then slick on a coat of clear mascara to add extra definition.

Top tip. Before your guests leave take a photo of each of them to show the quality of your salon. Pour everyone a cup of bedtime herbal tea so they're sure to enjoy a good night's sleep when they get home.

HOW TO CREATE YOUR OWN DRESSING TABLE

Create a little oasis of calm in your bedroom by organising all of your beauty goodies really nicely. Any table, shelf or windowsill will do – you could even set everything up on a tray covered with a piece of pretty fabric. Whatever you choose, the same rules apply.

- Too many things on display will look cluttered and gather dust. Keep your favourite items on show and store everything else in a selection of pretty boxes or bags – decorated margarine tubs and pencil cases are ideal.

- A cutlery tray makes it easy for you to organise all your stuff into sections – hair clips in one section, nail polish in another.

You can store it in a drawer or slide it under your bed and just bring it out whenever you need it.

• Try to get a good-sized mirror – it can be hand-held, free-standing or attached to a wall. You'll never look your best if you're constantly peering into a tiny compact-sized mirror.

• Make sure your dressing table is close to a good light source so that you can see what you're doing properly.

• Decorate your dressing table with a few pretty ornaments. Why not arrange shells from the seaside, a few wild flowers in a jam jar, or some cute trinkets from a charity shop?

HOW TO BEAT THE BLUES

Try one of these simple ideas to cheer yourself up the next time you're feeling a little down.

• Phone your best friend for a cheerful chat. Don't moan. Plan a great day out or weekend treat instead.

• Watch your favourite funny movie.

• Keep a memory box full of 'happy things'. A good rummage through old birthday cards, invitations and favourite photographs will clear the clouds.

• Put on your favourite music and dance away the blues.

• Pick some pretty flowers or interesting leaves and arrange them in a vase.

HOW TO CHOOSE THE PERFECT GLOVES

With so many options available it's difficult to know which glove to choose. Use this handy guide to help you select just the right one for any occasion.

- Long gloves, worn above the elbow, are perfect for a ball or other glamorous event but they will make it much more difficult to eat so make sure you have a snack before you go.

- Pink rubber gloves are essential for the washing-up to keep your hands looking gorgeous.

- At a wedding white lace is traditional, but can become itchy, so try to get satin instead whenever possible to prevent irritation.

- In winter, woollen gloves are best, but if you are somewhere particularly cold sheepskin mittens are ideal to help avoid chapped hands.

- If you're meeting the Queen opt for short silk gloves in case she wants to shake your hand.

HOW TO GET RID OF TANGLES

If your hair's really tangled up you'll need to take special care when you try to untangle the knots or you'll risk badly damaging your crowning glory.

1. Start by smoothing lots of conditioner over your hair – use olive oil if you haven't got conditioner.

2. Try to separate the strands using your fingers. Start at the ends of the hair and work up towards the roots. Keep going until you get most of the large knots out. Hold the hair near the scalp with one hand and use the other to untangle. That way, when you brush, there will be less pulling (and less pain).

3. Take a wide-toothed comb and work it gently through your hair from the bottom upwards. Rub conditioner over the teeth of the comb to help it glide through the hair really easily.

4. Finally, comb through the hair with a fine-toothed comb until all the tangles are removed.

5. Rinse out the conditioner once your hair is knot-free. Then shampoo and condition again.

Top tip. Do you wake up every morning with tangled hair? Try placing a rectangular silk scarf over your pillow while you sleep – it'll stop your hair fuzzing into knots.

HOW TO FRENCH PLAIT YOUR HAIR

This is a single braid that follows the curve of your head from the crown to the nape of your neck. A French plait is similar to a basic three-strand plait, except that you pick up extra strands of hair as you work your way down. As long as your hair is below chin-length you should be able to manage it. Get together with a friend and practise on each other.

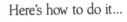

Here's how to do it...

1. Separate the hair from ear to ear, across the top of your friend's head. Gather the top section and divide it into three equal strands as though you're making an ordinary plait.

2. Start by crossing the right strand over the centre strand, then bring the left strand across, just as you would with a normal plait.

3. Before you plait the third strand scoop up an extra section of hair taken from the loose hair directly underneath.

4. Carry on plaiting, but from now on, add an extra section of hair to each strand as you go. Try to take a similar amount of hair each time to keep the plait even.

5. The plait will naturally follow the curve of her head as you pick up and include the new hair. Keep going until you reach the nape of the neck and all of the hair has been included.

6. Finish by plaiting the rest of the hair to the ends and secure it with a pretty hair elastic or a ribbon.

HOW TO GET RID OF FLAKY LIPS

Cold weather or nervous nibbling can lead to sore, dry lips. Here's a great way to make them better again.

• Slick your lips with petroleum jelly.

• Leave it on for ten minutes to soften any hard flakes of skin.

• Cover your index finger with a damp flannel and gently massage your lips. This will remove the petroleum jelly and the bits of dead skin at the same time.

• Rub a little petroleum jelly or lip salve into your lips to prevent the problem happening again.

HOW TO HAVE THE BEST MANNERS

Make the most of good manners with these helpful hints.

- No matter how hungry you are it's still rather rude to push into the queue for lunch. As a general rule there should be plenty of food to go around, so there's no rush.

- Losing can be a strain so try not to sulk if you don't win every time. It can be just as hard not to be a gloating winner, too, so remember to congratulate everyone else for playing well rather than laughing at the losers.

- Although it's tempting to jump straight onto the bus or train when seats are scarce, other travellers will always appreciate it if you let them get out first.

- If you're trying to win an argument you're much more likely to get positive results with cool reason rather than a hot temper. If you start to feel steam coming out of your ears try leaving your persuasion campaign until you've calmed down a little.

- If a friend or relative is nice enough to give you a present it's a good idea to have a polite response ready just in case you're not sure what it is. Say things like 'Oh, I love it!', 'I couldn't have thought of something so original' and 'That'll be really useful'. Say 'Thank you' straight away, especially if you need to call or write. If you forget you might not be so lucky next year!

If you can manage all of that you are definitely a glamorous goddess!

HOW TO ORDER FOOD
IN A RESTAURANT

If your family is going out for a special meal remember these top tips and you'll be able to order your food with style and ease.

- Don't be afraid to ask what something is if you are unsure – it's much better than getting a nasty surprise on your plate.

- Some restaurants have hundreds of items on the menu so don't bother to read the whole thing. Pick a section you like the look of and choose something from there.

- It's perfectly alright to order a drink first if you need more time to decide. Don't be rushed into ordering too soon.

- Take a peek at what people are eating at other tables. If they look as though they're enjoying their meal choose the same dish.

- Try not to order too much. There's nothing worse than over-indulging and feeling terrible afterwards.

- Be prepared to try something new – you might enjoy it.

Bon appetit!

HOW TO HAVE A WHITER SMILE

Sparkling teeth and fresh breath are a real beauty boost. These tips will help give you a head-start.

• Brush your teeth twice a day to remove plaque. This is the sticky layer that builds up on teeth and it is the main cause of tooth decay.

• Brush for at least two minutes each time. Hum along to some music while you do it to help pass the time more quickly.

• Don't forget to brush your tongue as well as your teeth. This will clear the surface of old food and help prevent bad breath.

• An old toothbrush can't do its job properly, so change yours every three months, or sooner if the bristles are splayed.

• Use dental floss regularly to clean between your teeth where your toothbrush just can't reach.

• Visit your dentist twice a year to make sure your teeth are in perfect health.

• A natural remedy for sweeter-smelling breath is to chew parsley leaves. They're rich in a chemical called 'chlorophyll' – Mother Nature's own deodorant.

- To help prevent tooth decay save sweets and sugary food and drink for an occasional treat.

- Keep your breath fresh by rinsing thoroughly with a mouthwash. You can make your own using a strong peppermint tea. Pour hot water over two tea bags and wait for it to cool before popping the cup in the fridge to chill.

- If you'd like really sparkling teeth you can even make your own whitening toothpaste. Baking soda has been used for years as a natural tooth whitener. It's really cheap and available in most supermarkets. Dip a dampened toothbrush into the soda, then gently brush your teeth to remove any stains and improve whiteness.

HOW TO LOOK BEAUTIFUL FOR FREE

The best three beauty treats of all are actually free – sleep, fresh air and lots of water.

- Breathing in fresh air literally oxygenates your skin so that it looks rosy and fresh.

- Most of us simply don't drink enough water. Two thirds of our bodies are made up of water.

- As well as boosting your energy levels, sleep gives your body the chance to repair and renew itself so you look even more beautiful the next morning.

HOW TO MAKE YOUR OWN JEWELLERY BOX

If you have lots of pretty bracelets, beads and rings you need somewhere special to keep them. It's easy to turn an old carton or container into your own decorated jewellery box.

What you'll need:

- An empty cardboard box – an old chocolate box is ideal.
- Various patterned papers to decorate with. Be as imaginative as you can. You could use pictures from old magazines and newspapers, old wrapping paper, used postage stamps, old musical scores or glittery stickers.
- Liquid PVA craft glue – the sort that dries clear.
- Fabric to line the box – anything from fun fur to velvet
- Scissors.

What to do:

1. Cut up your pieces of paper.

2. Glue the pieces of paper to the outside of the box, making sure they overlap. Keep going until the whole box is covered. If you want your box to look old, now's the time to 'age' the paper. While the glue is drying simply leave a tea bag in water for a few minutes, then brush the tea over the surface of the box and leave it to dry.

3. Brush a layer of glue all over the surface of the box. This helps protect the box and makes it look shinier.

4. Once the glue's dry on the outside it's time to decorate the

inside. Simply cut your chosen fabric to fit inside the base, sides and lid of your box and glue into place.

5. When it's dry, fill your new jewellery box with all your favourite trinkets.

HOW TO REMOVE INK STAINS FROM YOUR FINGERS

Oh no! You have an important birthday party to attend but your pen has leaked all over your hands. Inky fingers are okay for school but not so good for parties, but it's easy to bleach away the stains with an ordinary lemon. Just cut the lemon in half and rub the cut side over the ink stains. Wash your hands in gentle soap afterwards, then rub in some hand cream.

HOW TO LOOK (AND FEEL) PERKY WHEN YOU'RE FEELING TIRED

When you've got a busy day ahead but you wake up feeling exhausted, here's how to perk yourself up.

• Freshen up with a tingly lemon shower gel. If you can bear it, switch the water on to cold just before you finish showering for an ultra-invigorating start to your day.

• Wash your hair while you're in the shower. Take the time to massage your scalp with your fingertips. It's a great pick-me-up.

• Eat some breakfast – it really is the most important meal of the day and gives you the energy you need to get going. Try wholemeal toast and a glass of orange juice, or a bowl of unsweetened muesli with a chopped banana and yoghurt.

• Try this simple deep-breathing exercise to increase your energy levels. Lie on your back, supporting your head with a cushion, and place your hands on your tummy. Shut your eyes and concentrate on expanding your tummy as you breathe in, and flattening it as you breathe out. Continue for five minutes.

• Your body needs lots of fresh air and daylight, so take a brisk ten minute walk at some point in the day and drink plenty of water to refresh you.

• Put on the spritz with a fresh-smelling body spray. It will lift your spirits and make you smell great, too.

• Gently pinch your cheeks to give them a red glow that will make your look instantly healthier.

- Lie down and place a cold tea bag over each eye for five minutes. There is an ingredient called 'tannin' in tea, which reduces puffiness in your eyes and makes them look brighter.

HOW TO GIVE YOURSELF A FACE MASSAGE

Just like every part of your body, your face will look better after a mini massage.

- Pour a few drops of olive oil into your hands and smooth it onto your face and neck.

- Use your fingers to stroke upwards from the base of your neck to your chin.

- Now stroke up one side of your face, then the other.

- Go around your nose and up towards your forehead.

- Stroke across your forehead from left to right, using one hand.

- Finish off by gently 'drawing' a circle around each eye using one finger.

HOW TO DO A FRENCH MANICURE

When it comes to nail trends, there's one look that never goes out of fashion and that's the French manicure. It leaves your nails looking clean, fresh and healthy, and it matches any outfit.

Here's how to do it:

1. The classic French manicure uses two coats of pale pink polish. Look for a natural shade without any extra sparkly bits.

2. The best way to apply nail polish is in three strokes – one down the centre of the nail and one stroke either side. Apply two coats, giving each one plenty of time to dry.

Top tip. To turn a French manicure into an 'American manicure', use a beige polish instead of a pink one.

Paint one stroke down the centre then one either side.

3. Now it's time to paint the tips of your nails with a white polish. Be careful not to overload the brush or the varnish will flow down the bristles too quickly for you to control.

Top tip. Rest your hand on a firm surface to keep your hands steady and create a perfect finish.

Paint just the tip white.

4. Once the white tips of your nails are dry, paint on a clear topcoat of polish to seal in the colour and create a chip-free finish.

Top tip. If you're feeling impatient you can dry nail polish more quickly by blasting your nails with a cold jet of air from your hairdryer.

HOW TO LOOK YOUR BEST IN A PHOTOGRAPH

Make the most of any opportunity you get in front of a camera.
Practise these useful pointers to make sure you always look your best.

- Brush your hair quickly in case it's sticking up and check
that you don't have anything stuck between your teeth.

- Don't stand straight on to the camera, turn your body
slightly to one side, but keep your head facing forward for
a more natural pose.

- Don't look directly into the lens, look slightly to
the side instead – this will help to you avoid 'red eye'.

- Press your tongue to the roof of your mouth, lift your
chin slightly as though you are stretching to look over
a high garden fence and smile. This way you'll avoid any
unflattering shadows under your chin.

- If your photographer is using a flash widen your eyes a little
just before the picture is taken so that you're not caught
with your eyes closed.

- Try not to stand with your back to a light. You will only appear
in silhouette, which will defeat the object!

- People always look good in a photograph when they are
laughing – try to think of something funny just before the shot
and you'll be caught at your best possible moment.

HOW TO MAKE AN ACCEPTANCE SPEECH

You've finally been nominated for an award and, suddenly out of all the nominees, the host announces that you're the winner! You have a limited time to make a dazzling acceptance speech so make sure yours is the one that people are talking about the next day. Follow these pointers to make the most of your moment at the mic.

• If possible choose a fun way to get onto the stage – run across the seats, cartwheel, crowd-surf or dance – anything, as long as you make a lasting impression.

• Remember to mention that it's an honour to be singled-out from such a wonderful group of nominees.

• Tears are fine, but make sure everyone can still hear you.

• Memorise a short list of the most important people to thank and then say 'Everyone else – you know who you are'.

• When the music starts playing, leave the stage immediately.

Top tip. If you don't win, remember to plaster a delighted-looking smile on your face and applaud loudly till everyone stops looking.

HOW TO MAKE WELLINGTON BOOTS WORK FOR YOU

Wellington boots might seem like a fashion no-no but with a little creativity and panache you'll be able to carry off a long walk through muddy fields easily. These tips are guaranteed to help you stay stylish in the country or the city.

- Look out for all the trendy wellie designs from funky flowers to colourful rainbows – even celebrities are wearing them to brighten up their winter outfits.

- Alternatively you could funk up your old wellies by using water-proof pens or acrylic paints.

- Always try to match your outfit to your boots. If you can coordinate with extra accessories, even better.

Now even on the dullest day you'll be able to stay stylish and make the most boring wellies a fashion must-have.

HOW TO GIVE A GREAT INTERVIEW

If you're about to give an interview to a magazine or TV journalist, it's important to prepare in advance. Good tactics can make a big difference and help you to leave a great lasting impression.

• When you meet the interviewer order a long, cool drink, such as a smoothie, to stop your throat getting dry. It will also come in handy if you are asked any difficult questions – take a long sip of your drink while you come up with a good answer.

• Don't forget to look the interviewer straight in the eye when you meet them. Shake their hand firmly and smile confidently – that way they'll know how friendly and open you are.

• Name-dropping can be impressive. Mention your favourite celebrities by their first names to convince the interviewer that you're the best of friends.

• If you're about to appear in your school play or sing in a talent contest bring it up as often as you dare – the more publicity you can get, the better.

• People will soon get bored of hearing about you if you give hundreds of interviews. Only pick your favourite magazine or TV show to talk to and give them an 'exclusive' instead.

• Make sure everyone knows how to spell your name correctly.

HOW TO MAKE YOUR OWN SIGNATURE PERFUME

This is the simplest recipe ever for making perfume at home. Just use your favourite garden flowers and herbs.

What you'll need:

- 240 ml/1 cup of water
- 1 cup of fresh flower petals, chopped
- Muslin square (or, failing that, a clean cotton dishcloth)
- Bowl and saucepan
- Pretty bottle.

What to do:

1. Spread the muslin in the bowl, letting the edges hang over the rim.

2. Fill with the flower petals and cover them with water.

3. Cover with a plate and leave to stand overnight.

4. The next day, carefully lift the muslin cloth out of the bowl and squeeze the scented water into a saucepan.

5. Get an adult to help you gently heat the scented water until only about an egg-cup-full remains.

6. Leave to cool, then pour into your pretty bottle.

7. Dab on your perfume and smell gorgeous. (Kept in the fridge, this perfume should last up to a month.)

HOW TO BLOW-DRY YOUR HAIR PERFECTLY

Keep your hair looking sleek and shiny with a salon-style blow-dry at home. This step-by-step guide will help you get it right.

1. Comb your hair gently after shampooing and conditioning to remove any knots.

(See page 79 if your hair's in a real pickle.)

2. Gently squeeze your hair to remove excess water.

3. Wrap your hair up in a towel for five minutes.

4. Get to work with your hairdryer. Make sure you blow-dry down the length of the hair from the roots to the tips – this makes the outer 'cuticle' of each hair lie flat, which means shinier hair.

5. Work the hairdryer quickly over your head, ruffling your hair with your fingers at the same time.

6. Tip your head upside down while you direct the dryer's nozzle at the roots – this will build body into your hair.

7. Only when your hair is just beginning to feel dry, start using a brush to style it – before that, you're wasting your time.

8. Style the front of your hair first – it's the bit that everyone will notice. Work your way around to the sides and back. It may be helpful to use clips to section off parts of the hair you're not working on.

9. Give your hair a final blast of cool air to fix the style.

10. Ruffle with your fingers – to add a little texture.

HOW TO SMELL GORGEOUS

Nothing says glamour like smelling great. Try out these tactics and you'll always be the sweetest-smelling girl around.

FRESH AS A DAISY

It goes without saying, but you should have a bath or shower every single day.

HERBAL REMEDY

Add sprigs of herbs to your bath for a natural treat. Refreshing ones to try are mint, rosemary and thyme – either raid the kitchen cupboard for dried ones or check out the garden for fresh herbs. Once the tub is full, toss in the herbs and let them float in the water to release their scent.

FULL STEAM AHEAD

Adding a few drops of perfume to the floor of the shower will create beautifully scented steam.

A FRESH START

Sprinkle a dry towel with your favourite fresh fragrance. Put it in the tumble dryer for a few minutes until it heats up and give yourself a vigorous rubdown. The hot fragranced towel will make you feel fabulously awake and alert.

SWEET DREAMS

Sprinkle your bedsheets with talcum powder! You'll wake up smelling lovely.

EAT THAI

Smell sweet with Thai food. Believe it or not, this type of food is said to produce the nicest body smells, so take the opportunity to eat lots of it! It contains plenty of aromatic ingredients, such as mint, lemon grass and coconut. Go easy on the garlic, though!

LAYERS OF LOVELINESS

Learn to layer fragrance to smell beautiful all day. Start with a scented bath oil, and soap. Move on to the body lotion and finish with *eau de toilette*. Put a perfume gift set on your next birthday or Christmas wish-list.

HOW TO TIE-DYE A T-SHIRT

The best way to brighten up a boring old white T-shirt is by tie-dyeing it. It's much easier than it looks to create a groovy sunburst design and add some hippy chic to your wardrobe.

What you'll need:

- A pack of cold-water dye in any colour you fancy
- Salt and a metal spoon
- Elastic bands to create the designs
- Rubber gloves to stop the dye staining your hands
- One measuring jug filled with cold water
- One washing-up bowl filled with warm water
- One white T-shirt (obviously!).

Top tip. Check that it's okay to use things from the kitchen before you start, or buy your own set specially for dyeing.

Here's how:

1. Prepare the mixture – open the dye container and pour the powder into the jug of cold water. Let it dissolve.

2. Add the bag of fixative and the required amount of salt. (Every brand of dye is slightly different, so read the instructions carefully.) Stir until everything's dissolved.

3. Pour the dye mixture into the bowl of warm water. Stir again until thoroughly mixed.

4. To prepare the T-shirt, in the middle of the front. an elastic band around the sections of fabric covered bands won't absorb the dy remain white.

5. Next, bunch the fabric together and tie a second elastic band around the pinch about 5 cm from the first.

6. Continue adding elastic bands, 5 cm apart, until the front of the T-shirt is completely wrapped.

7. If you like, repeat the same process again on the back of the T-shirt and even on the sleeves of the T-shirt.

8. Immerse your T-shirt in the bowl of dye. Push it down into the liquid with the spoon to make sure it's thoroughly wet.

9. Leave your T-shirt to soak for an hour then squeeze out the water and rinse away any excess dye.

10. Hang the T-shirt up on a line to dry, then remove the elastic bands. *Voilà*, a beautiful sunburst T-shirt.

HOW TO SOOTHE TIRED FEET

It's no surprise that at the end of a hard day at school (or at the shops) your feet can feel tired and sore. Try this quick and simple remedy to bring them back to life.

Start by soaking your feet in a bowl of warm water to which you've added a handful of sea salt. Keep them there for five minutes. Next, try lying down on your back on the floor with your feet up, resting on the edge of the sofa. Stay there for ten minutes.

HOW TO MAKE A DOOR CURTAIN

Create a glamorous entrance to your bedroom with a beaded door curtain. It looks fab and is easy to make.

What You'll Need:

- Thick piece of ribbon cut to the same width as your doorframe.
- About 30 plastic straws – any colour.
- 12 pieces of fishing line or strong clear thread, each 1.8 m long.
- Plastic beads – around 200.
- A few drawing pins to secure the curtain to your doorframe.
- Scissors.

How To Make It:

1. Lay the thick piece of ribbon on the floor. Secure each strand of fishing line to the ribbon at equal intervals – do this by looping one end of the thread over the ribbon and tying a knot.

2. Cut the straws into 5 cm lengths.

3. String the beads and straw pieces onto each length of fishing line, alternating them and finishing with a bead.

4. When the fishing line is full, feed the end of the thread through the bead twice – finish with a knot to secure in place.

5. Repeat for each piece of fishing line.

6. Get an adult to tack the curtain over your door with drawing pins.

HOW TO LIP-SYNCH SUCCESSFULLY

If you haven't got a good singing voice but want to become a pop star it's important to learn how to lip-synch. This is a kind of miming where you look as if you're singing a song even when you're not. Here are some tips to help you.

• Choose a simple song that you can really put your heart and soul into. Look for one that is funny, or very emotional, or which has a strong beat.

• Learn the lyrics! There's nothing worse than forgetting the words mid-performance.

• Really think about what the words of the song mean and aim to express this with your body language during your show.

• Don't be afraid to exaggerate your facial movements during your performance – the audience will really enjoy it.

• Dress up – it will really boost your confidence.

- Never turn your back on your audience – it will make it more difficult to keep their attention.

- Don't worry if you think people suspect you're lip-synching – some of the most famous singers do it. Concentrate on performing it as well as you can.

- If you're not confident enough to perform alone, get a friend or a group of friends to join you. There are plenty of duets and songs by bands to choose from.

HOW TO BE THE COOLEST PARTY GUEST

Follow these simple rules to take the party world by storm.

- Always be fashionably late – twenty minutes or so is ideal. After all, this party is just one of many on your social calendar. (Don't be too late though, you don't want to appear rude.)

- Smile and look around at everyone when you enter a room – even if you don't know anyone it will make people want to come and talk to you.

- Mingle with as many people as possible. Next time people will notice if you're not there and you'll probably end up with even more party invitations.

- Don't be the last to leave – even the best party girl has to get enough beauty sleep!

HOW TO MAKE A BUTTON AND BEAD CHARM BRACELET

What you'll need:

• A selection of pretty buttons. (Ask an adult if you can raid their sewing box for some, snip them off old, unwanted clothes, or scour charity shops and sewing stores for bargains.)

• A selection of pretty beads.

• Some elastic thread.

• Sewing thread, cut into 10 cm lengths.

What to do:

1. Measure enough elastic to fit around your wrist and then add on 8 cm extra. Knot the ends together and snip away any excess.

2. Take one bead or button at a time, and feed a length of sewing thread through its hole. Then secure on the thread with a knot.

3. Now tie the button or bead around the elastic. Secure with a double knot and snip off the excess thread.

4. Keep on adding buttons and beads until you can't see the elastic any more.

Top tip. Cram as many buttons and beads onto the elastic as you can. The more they overlap, the better the bracelet will look.

HOW TO LOOK INSTANTLY TALLER

Good posture is the best way to add inches to your height. It'll make you look more confident, too. Look in a mirror and check yourself out.

- DO keep your neck straight from hairline to shoulders.

- DON'T let your head hang forward.

- DO keep your chest high and your shoulder blades flat.

- DON'T hunch up your shoulders or slump forward.

- DO stand tall with a shallow curve in the small of your back.

- DON'T stick your tummy out.

- DO tuck your bottom in.

- DON'T stand with your feet turned out – keep them parallel with each other.

HOW TO WRITE YOUR FIRST AUTOBIOGRAPHY

An autobiography is a real-life story, which you write all about yourself and your life. It is a great way to tell fans how you became famous, so it is a good idea to start making notes now.

- Keep a journal. When you look back you'll be able to remember exactly how you were feeling each day and use it to add lots of emotional touches to your story.

- Read the autobiography of someone you admire for inspiration.

- Ask your family and friends for any funny anecdotes they can remember about your early years. These are especially good if they show how talented you were, even as a baby.

- Remember to be totally honest. It's almost certain that someone will know if you have exaggerated anything, which could lead to embarrassment later on.

- Aim to have your first autobiography completed by the age of 16. That way you'll still have plenty of time to write the second and third volumes.

HOW TO PRETEND YOU CAN DANCE FLAMENCO

Fool people that you can dance the flamenco with this mini-routine. Get your friends to clap their hands rhythmically while you perform these moves as dramatically as you can.

1. Stand as tall as you can. Reach up with your right arm and pretend you're plucking an apple from a high branch of a tree. Hold the imaginary apple with the very tips of your fingers.

2. Now you must pretend you are going to take a bite from the apple. Rotate your wrist clockwise as you bend your elbow and bring your imaginary apple towards your mouth (don't actually bite).

3. Now start swinging your hips, stomping your feet and turning in circles.

4. Pretend to throw the apple to the ground, a look of utter disgust on your face.

5. Now stamp on the imaginary apple, moving your feet faster and faster as you crush it to a pulp.

6. Repeat.

HOW TO EAT SPAGHETTI LIKE A REAL ITALIAN

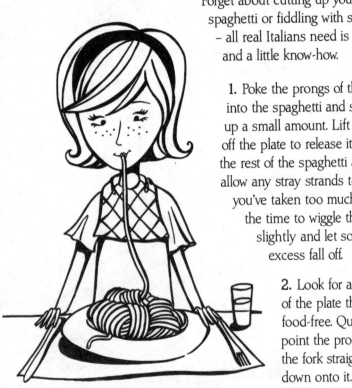

Forget about cutting up your spaghetti or fiddling with spoons – all real Italians need is a fork and a little know-how.

1. Poke the prongs of the fork into the spaghetti and scoop up a small amount. Lift it high off the plate to release it from the rest of the spaghetti and to allow any stray strands to fall. If you've taken too much, now's the time to wiggle the fork slightly and let some excess fall off.

2. Look for an area of the plate that's food-free. Quickly point the prongs of the fork straight down onto it.

3. Twirl the fork a few times to create a roll of strands.

4. Quickly flick your wrist and place the rolled-up spaghetti into your mouth. *Bravo!*

HOW TO DRESS TO SUIT YOUR STAR SIGN

Each star sign is said to have its own special fashion style. Check out the looks linked to your star sign and see if it sounds like you.

ARIES – MARCH 21ST TO APRIL 20TH

You're a trend-setter – always willing to try new looks. You've got brilliant fashion radar and you know whether an outfit's going to become a hit or a miss. Your favourite colours are red and black.

TAURUS – APRIL 21ST TO MAY 21ST

You'd rather snap up a vintage cashmere jumper for a few pounds than spend the same amount on a cheap high-street T-shirt. You love subtle, expensive shades of brown, khaki and cream.

GEMINI – MAY 22ND TO JUNE 21ST

You get bored hanging on to any outfit for too long. You mix and match styles and love shimmery fabrics and coloured patterns.

CANCER – JUNE 22ND TO JULY 23RD

You love comfortable, feminine clothes – soft jumpers and floaty skirts. If you find a piece of clothing you like, you keep it in your wardrobe for years. You love to dress in soft blues and greens.

LEO – JULY 24TH TO AUGUST 23RD

You wear anything that makes a statement – from flowing tops to nipped-in jackets. You love gold, red, bronze and orange.

VIRGO – AUGUST 24TH TO SEPTEMBER 23RD

Virgo is the best-turned-out star sign of all – you'll spend a lot of time taking care of your clothes. You love neat and tidy looks and soft fabrics with natural colours like green, grey and brown.

LIBRA – SEPTEMBER 24TH TO OCTOBER 23RD

You've got great taste and favour classical looks. Somehow, though, you always manage to put an outfit together that looks up-to-date and modern. You opt for rich blues, dark pinks and black.

SCORPIO – OCTOBER 24TH TO NOVEMBER 22ND

One day you're super-smart, the next barefoot and natural – a real mixture. The colours you keep coming back to are black and red.

SAGITTARIUS – NOVEMBER 23RD TO DECEMBER 21ST

You love colourful, casual clothes that let you move, and you don't really care what others think of you. You prefer soft, natural fibres in earthy shades of purple, green and dark blue.

CAPRICORN – DECEMBER 22ND TO JANUARY 20TH

You're not a label snob – as long as you like an outfit, you don't care how much it costs or what range it comes from. Colour-wise, you favour charcoal grey, brown and black.

AQUARIUS – JANUARY 21ST TO FEBRUARY 19TH

You're unconventional with clothes and your friends often look to you for a hint of what style might be in next. You experiment with colour but always find yourself coming back to blue.

PISCES – FEBRUARY 20TH TO MARCH 20TH

You would happily buy all your clothes from a second-hand shop but when you dress up you can look as good as anyone. Your favourite colours are silver, purple and cream.

HOW TO WALK IN HIGH-HEELED SHOES

High-heeled shoes look lovely if you're off to a party or a wedding but they can be tricky to walk in at first. Follow this simple guide and you'll soon be skipping around like a real lady.

- Choose a low heel or a wedge (where the gap between the heel and toe is filled in) so that you can practise walking more easily – don't aim too high at first.

- Find a good place to practise where you have plenty to hold on to and stand up slowly and carefully. Your centre of gravity will be higher than usual so flex each knee a little to steady yourself.

- Keep your bottom tucked in and balance on the balls of your feet. Take a few steps placing each heel first before putting your toe down. Be careful not to get a heel caught in the carpet.

- Keep practising at home for a couple of days until you feel ready to go out. Try a short trip around the corner and back before attempting a longer outing. Soon you'll be able to run for a bus with ease.

Top tip. Take a spare pair of flat shoes along, too, just in case you get tired.

HOW TO FIND THE PERFECT PERFUME

There are thousands of perfumes in the shops, which means it can be hard to whittle them down to find the one you really like and which most suits your personality.

TRIAL AND ERROR

• Head for the perfume counter at a department store or a large chemist for the best choice. Try a maximum of three – your nose will get tired and they will all start to smell the same.

• Start by taking a look at the ingredients before you spritz. If you're quite girly you might love floral perfumes. If you're sporty, citrus scents like lemon or grapefruit could be ideal.

• Spray a little onto the inside of your wrist or elbow, then wait ten minutes for the perfume to 'develop' properly. You shouldn't buy a perfume even if you like it straight away. Perfumes often smell quite different after a couple of hours. If you like the way it smells on your skin later on in the day, you're on to a winner.

HOW TO WEAR IT

The best place to wear a perfume is on one of your pulse points – where the blood is closest to your skin's surface. These include your temples, the side of your neck (not behind your ears!), in the crook of your elbow, your inner wrists, the backs of your knees and on the front of your ankles. Some perfumers recommend spritzing freshly washed hair so that you waft a delicious scent around you as you move your head.

HOW TO MAKE A MOOD BOARD

The most glamorous girls always know what suits them, as well as the styles and colours they really love. You can work out your own personal style, too, by creating a 'Mood Board' for your bedroom.

First of all, you'll need a pin board for the wall. If you haven't got one of these, try securing four cork floor tiles to your wall with sticky tac.

Now the fun bit... start collecting clippings from fashion magazines, photos, old postcards, adverts, paint swatches, fabric scraps, leaves – anything at all. The only important thing is that you really love everything. Take your time deciding which things really appeal to you. Spread them out on your bed while you decide. You may be able to gather them into little sections of similar colours or style.

Once you're happy with your selection, arrange them onto your pin board. Now sit back and take a look – your personal taste will be there for you to admire whenever you want.

HOW TO SEEM CONFIDENT WHEN YOU'RE NOT

The next time you're feeling shy and overwhelmed, try out these DOs and DON'Ts to make others think you're feeling completely confident...

• DON'T wear dull colours.
Instead of trying to blend in with the background, get yourself noticed by wearing confident reds, oranges or yellows.

• DO get your body language right.
Hold your head high however nervous you feel. Don't clasp your hands in front of you or fold them – it's much better to stand with your arms hanging relaxed and loose at your sides. Sit with your hands resting loosely in your lap.

• DON'T hide behind your hair.
Let people see your face – hair swept back into a neat ponytail says that you're okay about people looking at you.

• DO smile.
People often confuse shyness with unfriendliness – a smile shows you're friendly and makes people feel relaxed around you.

• DON'T talk too quickly.
Relax and take a deep breath. Take your time and give yourself a chance to think about what you want to say. Avoid just blurting out the first thing that comes into your head.

• DO look people in the eye.
One of the most obvious signs of shyness is when you avoid making eye contact with the person you're talking to.

• DON'T chew your nails.
Nibbling on fingers is a dead give-away that you're feeling nervous.

• DO lift your spirits with scent.
Apply a dot of grapefruit or bergamot essential oil on your wrists before heading out the door in the morning. They're great for boosting your confidence and you can take a quick sniff whenever you need a boost.

HOW TO STRIKE A POSE

When everyone is looking your way it's vital to make sure that your every move seems as naturally glamorous as possible, whether you've just popped to the corner shop or you're making a brief appearance at a film premier. Next time you're on the red carpet try out these top moves.

THE HAIR FLIP

As you step onto the school bus smile, wave and flip your head up so that your hair swishes out behind you. Try not to catch yourself in the eye though, as this will sting.

THE LOOK BEHIND YOU

Walk past your waiting photographers without stopping. Just when they think you've ignored them completely stop, put one hand on your hip and look back over your shoulder before giving them your best smile.

THE BIG TUMBLE

This one is usually best avoided but it's important to be prepared so that you can gracefully jump straight back up again if you fall.

Now practise, practise, practise...

HOW TO EMPHASISE YOUR EYE COLOUR

A great way to make your natural eye colour really stand out for parties is to wear clothes in just the right shade. Forget about wearing blues if you have blue eyes, and browns if you have brown eyes – these are the best choices...

Eye Colour: pale blue
Try: lilac or pastel pink

Eye Colour: mid-to-dark blue
Try: peach or gold

Eye Colour: light brown
Try: honey brown or khaki green

Eye Colour: dark brown
Try: toffee brown or olive green

Eye Colour: pale green
Try: lavender or blue-grey

Eye Colour: dark green
Try: peach or plum

Eye Colour: hazel
Try: moss green or purple.

HOW TO BEAD YOUR HAIR

Beaded hair looks really pretty and costs just pennies. It only takes a little time and practice to achieve.

You'll need:

- A handful of beads with large holes. Plastic ones are best as they're lighter – you don't want to be too weighed down.

- A reel of cotton, any colour.

How to do it:

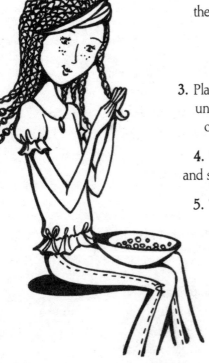

1. Pick up a strand of hair about the thickness of a shoelace.

2. Divide it into three smaller strands.

3. Plait the three strands together until you have about 5 cm of hair left at the ends.

4. Wet the end of the plait and smooth the ends together.

5. Thread a bead onto the plait and push it up the hair.

6. Add as many beads as you like, carefully pushing each one up the plait.

7. When you've finished, wind a length of cotton around the

end of the plait and tie in place. Alternatively, use
a thin hairband, if you prefer.

8. Repeat the whole process to make as many plaits
as you like. You could even enlist some friends
to help you bead all of your hair.

HOW TO TELL WHAT THE SHAPE OF YOUR LIPSTICK MEANS

Raid your friends' make-up bags, whip out their used lipsticks or
lipbalms and explain how the shape of the tip reveals loads about
their personalities.

FLAT TOP

You're dependable and don't mess around. You care what people
think about you.

CONCAVE TOP

This bowl-shape means you're friendly, exciting and love a dare.

SLANTED TOP

If the end is close to its original shape, you probably stick to the
rules and don't like too much attention.

ROUNDED TOP

You're a loveable, friendly person who enjoys being busy.

POINTED TOP

You're kind and easygoing and can be relied on in a crisis.

HOW TO LOOK AFTER YOUR SKIN IN SUMMER

Everyone loves a day at the beach in Summer – but no one likes getting burnt by the sun. Check out this safe tan plan.

- Apply suntan lotion (SPF 15 or higher) first thing in the morning before getting dressed – that way you won't miss any areas.

- Lips are especially prone to burning and chapping in the sun – so slick on some lip salve.

- Stay out of the sun between 12 noon and 3 o'clock when the sun is at its hottest. Move into the shade or cover up with a T-shirt and a broad-brimmed hat.

- If you're a sporty type or fancy a cooling dip in the sea, choose a special waterproof sun lotion.

HOW TO LOOK AFTER YOUR SKIN IN WINTER

• Chilly temperatures and cold winds can make your skin dry and itchy. Always protect yourself with warm mittens, cosy scarves and cute hats.

• Dress in layers that will keep you warm from top to toe. Light cotton next to the skin helps keep your skin warm and dry.

• Bathe or shower in lukewarm water. Hot baths may sound nice but the heat can dry out the natural oils in your skin making it even itchier than before.

• Don't lick sore lips to try and soothe them, you'll make them even flakier. Slick on some balm or petroleum jelly instead.

HOW TO ESCAPE A HORDE OF FANS

It's difficult to be polite and glamorous all the time, so if you just need some time to yourself use these top tips to get away from the crowds.

• Kit yourself out with a brilliant disguise.
A wig and dark glasses are a great way to start but don't go overboard. A wooden leg and a parrot will only draw more attention to you.

• Get to know your route home like the back of your hand. Try to plan a clever detour and give everyone the slip when they least expect it.

• Perfect your celebrity-style wave. It's best performed getting into of an expensive car, but the school bus will do at a pinch. Walk quickly with your head down. Just before you get on, stop and turn to face your 'fans'. Raise your arm briefly and flash a quick smile. Remember – the more excited your fans are, the more disinterested your wave should be. Now turn and enter the bus, refusing, all autographs.

• Come up with a false name – the name of your favourite cartoon combined with your first pet is a simple way of doing this. Use it whenever you travel to avoid detection.

• If you find your exit blocked by autograph-hunters at your local café politely ask the owner if you can go through the kitchen instead and leave via the back door.

HOW TO TAKE CHARGE OF OUT-OF-CONTROL HAIR

The weather can wreak havoc on your hair. If your pretty curls have a case of the frizzies, or fly-away static is ruining your lovely tresses, try these helpful hints to take your hair in hand:

• **Frizzy.** Use a conditioner each time you wash your hair to keep it as sleek as possible – save lots of time with a spray-on and leave-in brand.

• **Frizzy.** Use your fingers as styling tools instead of brushes and combs – you're less likely to create frizz.

• **Frizzy.** Rub a few drops of almond oil between your palms, then smooth over your hair to combat crazy curls.

• **Fly-away.** Dry winter air can literally make your hair stand on end – use a wooden brush to help reduce static electricity.

• **Fly-away.** Use a moisturising shampoo and conditioner to stop your hair drying out.

• **Fly-away.** Spritz anti-static hairspray onto your brush before styling your hair.

HOW TO CHOOSE THE RIGHT SUNGLASSES FOR YOUR FACE SHAPE

Choosing the right pair of shades to suit your face shape can transform your whole look and give you just the right finishing touch. Check out how to work out your face shape on page 40, then decide which frames would suit you the best.

ROUND-SHAPED FACE

Look for broad styles which are equal to the width of your face. Square lenses look good, too.

HEART-SHAPED FACE

Delicate or rimless frames suit your pretty face shape perfectly. Angular shapes are also a good choice for you.

SQUARE-SHAPED FACE

Soft, gently curved, oval-shaped frames soften your defined features perfectly.

OVAL-SHAPED FACE

Lucky thing – everything suits you!

HOW TO BE A GODDESS

Owing to the goddess-like status you have now achieved by reading this book, you'll need to learn how to cope with the stresses and strains this role may bring.

• If you really want to look like a goddess borrow an old, white sheet and drape it around yourself in the style of a Roman toga.

• Wind some pretty flowers through your hair and always remember to leave a trail of blossoms wherever you walk.

• Smile gently at all times to give people the impression that you're calm and serene.

• If people are nice enough to offer you gifts, do your best to accept them with good manners (even if you'd rather they hadn't bothered).

• One of the best goddess skills you will learn is wisdom. Use it well and try to give the best advice you can.

• Most importantly – never abuse your powers.

ALSO AVAILABLE...

The Girls' Book: How To
Be The Best At Everything
ISBN: 978-1-905158-79-9

The Boys' Book of Survival:
How To Survive
Anything, Anywhere
ISBN: 978-1-906082-12-3

The Boys' Book: How To
Be The Best At Everything
ISBN: 978-1-905158-64-5

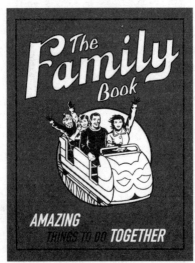

The Family Book:
Amazing Things To Do Together
ISBN: 978-1-906082-10-9